Goddess Love Oracle

Wendy Andrew

ROCKPOOL

A Rockpool book
PO Box 252
Summer Hill NSW 2130
Australia

rockpoolpublishing.com
Follow us! **f** **◎** rockpoolpublishing
Tag your images with #rockpoolpublishing

ISBN 978-1-925924-32-9

Edited by Lisa Macken
Designed by Jessica Le, Rockpool Publishing

Printed and bound in China
10 9 8 7 6 5 4

CONTENTS

INTRODUCTION

I would like to introduce myself to you and thank you so much for purchasing the *Goddess Love Oracle*.

I am an artist, dreamer and lover of Goddess. It is Her loving spirit that runs through us all, joining our hands together and linking our hearts. Through these cards I hope you will feel Her love. In those times when you feel disconnected, alone or unloved, let Her guide you back into the flow of Her unconditional love.

We share this beautiful planet with many other non-human brothers and sisters: creatures that bare no grudges and live in the moment; creatures that have many lessons to teach us about love and trust. Goddess will bring these creatures into your life, as and when you need encouragement, to help you on your journey of self-discovery and self-love.

I hope the paintings and words in this oracle will open your heart to the presence of Goddess in your life, so that She may bless you with all the acceptance, fulfilment, peace and love you deserve.

Special thanks to Tom Powell, NLP and life coach, for his inspired contribution to the writing for this oracle (www.tompowellcoaching.co.uk).

HOW TO USE THE CARDS

These oracle cards have been created with love and offer you the opportunity to be guided to a place within yourself where love resides. There are no hard and fast rules about how to use the cards; simply do what feels right and that will be Goddess guiding you. Allow yourself to feel the essence of Her messages as Her love enfolds you.

A quiet, undisturbed place and time will make it easier to be receptive to Her message. You may also like to cleanse the space and your aura of any negative energy by smudging with white sage or other incense. Ask for Her blessing on your use of the cards and that Her guidance will be received unhindered and acted on for the greater good of all beings.

You might like to sit quietly for a while holding the cards. Perhaps close your eyes and say: 'Goddess, I ask for Your blessings on my use of these cards. May I receive Your guidance clearly. May Your love fill my heart for the greater good of all.' When you are ready, if it feels right, you can shuffle the cards and tune into their vibration.

If you have a specific question, ask it now.

Whatever the reason that Goddess has called you here, offer it to Her. If you are suffering grief, loss or loneliness, She will hear you. Perhaps you are in need of inspiration or your life just isn't feeling right; let Her speak to you through the cards. You are Her dear one and She will help you.

There are many different ways of laying the cards, but here are a few suggestions.

Single-card reading

As you shuffle the cards let one present itself to you. You may like to fan out the cards face down and run your fingers over them until one calls to you. Turn it over and let Goddess speak to you through the image and words. Your instant reaction may be very valuable in understanding the advice and help being given. Very often your body will act as an amplifier to the subtle voice of spirit, so be aware of your physical reactions no matter how small. When you have absorbed the image and words on the card you can read the words in the accompanying guidebook, which will expand the message.

If you feel you would like to spend more time with the card place it on your altar, if you have one, or in a special place. Just make sure it is somewhere you will see it regularly to allow the Goddess's message to sink into your being.

This single-card reading can be done daily, weekly or monthly. It is, of course, much more beneficial to practise the pre-reading preparation and meditation, but if time does not allow for this then do let Goddess speak to you through a drawn card wherever or whenever you need help. You may find that a card drawn in a rush does not bring as clear a message; however, perhaps in a moment of quiet later on the image or words may come back to you and you will hear Her voice of wisdom!

If you don't have a specific question or dilemma that needs clarification, this is a lovely morning practice. Light a candle and sit for a moment with the cards. Ask Goddess to please light your path today with Her wisdom. Draw a card and let Her guidance enrich your day.

Three-card spread

There are many different ways of using the three-card spread. Following are two to begin with, but you may find that you develop your own.

As before, centre yourself with some long slow breaths and gently shuffle the cards. Be clear in your mind about the matter you would like Goddess guidance on. When you feel ready, lay out three cards from left to right.

Work, play and people spread: this spread can be done as a daily practice. Ask Goddess to guide you during the day in these specific areas of your life.

Card 1 represents the work aspect of your life. Goddess may guide you to approach your work with fresh eyes and renewed enthusiasm, or She may have a message of acceptance and calm.

Card 2 represents the downtime in your day. Listen to Her advice; you may perhaps need to make more time for play, self-development, meditation, exercise, self-care or fun!

Card 3 represents people or, more specifically, the way you interact with them.

Body, mind and spirit spread: this spread is particularly useful if you are feeling stuck and would like to ask Goddess for help in moving forward.

I suggest laying card 1 on the left, card 2 to the far right and card 3 in the centre. Read the cards in the order they were laid, with spirit being the last to be read.

Card 1 represents your body. You may find guidance in how to best look after your body to feel well and be able to deal better with life.

Card 2 represents your mind. Here Goddess may guide you to be kinder to yourself or to be more positive in your thought processing.

Card 3 represents your spirit. Be open to divine guidance and remember you are not alone, as Goddess is with you.

***

I hope your *Goddess Love Oracle* cards bring you insight, inspiration and pleasure and help bring you closer to Goddess. Let Her speak to you through the images and words.

Each card reading also comes with a suggested Goddess-inspired daily practice that will be helpful and may deepen your connection to the divine spirit that flows through you, bringing you peace and love.

Remember to keep alert to any synchronicities that may occur. For example, you may have drawn a card featuring a fox and later that day you pick up a book with a fox on the cover, or you receive a card in the post featuring a fox or you dream about a fox. These may not be mere coincidences but subtle nudges from Goddess to heed Her message.

You may also like to use the accompanying guidebook on its own; you can pop it into your bag or pocket when you go out. If you have a quick question or need a little inspiration, intuitively open the book and Goddess will guide you to the right page.

May Goddess bless you with clarity, enlightenment and love.

1.
AUTHENTICITY
Let your truth be heard

Rhiannon comes to you now, telling you to step into your own authenticity. You may feel a conflict within yourself that comes from stepping outside your deeply held values and beliefs in an attempt to fit in and be like others. Goddess calls you to step back into your own values. Own them; let them be as much a part of you as your heart is to your blood and your lungs are to your breath. Let your emotions, words and actions be as one.

Let them be guided by the gentle wisdom of Goddess. Let Her love and compassion for all things enter your being and you will move in alignment with your soul. This is authenticity.

Travel your path with your head held high and speak your truth. Let your emotions into your words and let your actions tell the story of love. Goddess's white mare will be your guide.

Walk with confidence. Do not be afraid to acknowledge your mistakes along the way. Listen and learn and, if needed, have the courage to apologise and change. Have faith in your dreams. If they are in alignment with the Goddess way of purity, kindness and love, they will come to fruition. Call on Rhiannon, Goddess of creativity, to help you manifest your true potential.

Now is the time for you to find new ways to show your true values and stand in your own truth. Rhiannon will give you courage to connect with the parts of yourself you have kept hidden. Let your inner light shine; let your truth be heard and your authenticity be shown.

💜 *Goddess-inspired daily practice:* make a list of your top 10 values, and see if they have a hierarchy of importance to you. To do this, ask yourself: 'What is important to me about life?' A clear value tends to be abstract, consist of just several words and not linked to a specific context, thing or person. Freedom, playfulness, contribution, tranquillity and compassion are all examples of values. Once you have your list, reflect on it each morning and night. Ask yourself what you are doing that either meets your values or doesn't meet your values. This will clearly guide you away from internal conflict and towards further authenticity.

2.

AWAKENING

Live in the moment

Brigid comes with Her sacred gift of awakening.
There are aspects and elements in your life
that are lying dormant, but perhaps you are not
even aware of their presence as they have been
asleep for so long. Once they have been stirred
into action you will wonder how you ever lived
without them! This awakening may be a slow
and challenging process, like struggling from
the depths of a warm and cozy slumber, or it may
be quick like a cold shower shocking you back

into awareness. Brigid may deliver Her gift as a message straight to your heart, and you will know that you will never be the same again.

Goddess Brigid knows the perfect time to bring you Her gift; She has been watching and waiting. Just as She knows when to wake the sleeping winter world at Imbolc, She knows when you are ready. She asks for nothing from you except your readiness. Relax and stop grasping. Surrender yourself to the flow of life. A dancer does not dance in order to get to the end of the music to discover its meaning; she feels and responds to every beat and note as she dances. In the same way, Goddess asks that you become aware of the countless magical moments in your everyday life, as it is your awareness of these small moments of magic that will indicate your readiness and your ability to really feel the music of life. Are you ready to be fully awake?

Brigid may send you Her sacred swan as a messenger to say 'live in the moment' and hare may come to remind you to be aware, accept and love.

💜 *Goddess-inspired daily practice:* whenever you find yourself exerting effort in trying to get to the end of something, ask yourself: 'How can I bring my attention to enjoying what I have right now?' Whenever you find yourself desiring a certain outcome, ask yourself: 'What would happen if I released rather than strived?'

3.

BLISS

Open your door to the Divine

Goddess comes to you saying: 'My gift to you is bliss. I offer you many ways to find happiness and delight in your life but you must put them into practice.' Perhaps you have intended to meditate regularly but just haven't found the time, or you meant to sit and eat your meals mindfully but instead gulp them down thoughtlessly while watching television. Maybe you sometimes think it would be nice to go for a quiet walk and smell the flowers but instead get involved with something else and say to yourself, 'I don't have time for that.'

Goddess comes to tell you that you do have time! Making space in your life to feel the presence of the Divine is all important. She can speak to you most clearly when you open the door for Her to come in. In giving yourself quiet time you open that door, Goddess will fill you up with Her radiance so you glow with the joy of life. She will show you how to love yourself, and in accepting and loving yourself you are showing your gratitude to Her.

She may send you one of Her sacred creatures to remind you to be still. Look out for Her little reminders and heed Her call. Make space in your busy life to let Goddess bring you Her gift of bliss.

💜 *Goddess-inspired daily practice:* give yourself at least 15 minutes every day for a quiet practice of some kind. It might be meditation, a mindful walk, a yoga practice or simply sitting with a cup of tea with no other distractions. When you notice your resistance towards entering into this practice, listen to what the resistance has to tell you and remind yourself of the bliss you can create for yourself. If you constantly find it hard to make time for yourself it may be useful to get out a pen and paper and write down the answers to these questions: 'By saying "no" to giving myself time for creating my own internal bliss, what am I saying yes to?', and 'By saying yes to [insert habit such as work, lying in bed], what am I saying "no" to?' It is likely you will find your answers very enlightening and motivating.

4.

CALMNESS
Let things settle

Life can sometimes be like rolling waves and
gusty winds that can leave you either energised
or exhausted and windswept! Times of great
movement and change can be thrilling: a stormy
sea will drag away sands and expose treasures
hiding just below and its currents will let new
opportunities rise to the surface. But to allow these
opportunities to manifest you need to examine the
treasures and quantify the opportunities.

Mother Ocean comes to offer you a period of
calmness and stillness, a chance to take stock and let

things settle. The world around you may be moving at a pace of a roaring tempest, but let your body and mind be still so that you may hear the gentle beating of your own heart pulsing the calming waves within you and the voice of Goddess guiding you. Her sacred seal teaches you to reveal your creative talents and let your imagination swim free.

The most precious treasure is to be found in the arms of Mother Ocean. You will feel Her gift of tranquillity seep into the depths of your inner sea, a space that resonates with the very truth of you. Here you know that you are whole, that you are loved and that you are in exactly the time and space that you need to be right now.

💜 *Goddess-inspired daily practice:* this is known as ocean (or Ujjayi) breath:

Breathe deeply in through your nose for a count of five, taking the air down into your belly and letting it expand. As you do so, tighten the muscles in the back of your throat to slightly restrict the flow of air.

- Exhale long, slowly and fully, using the same technique as above in your throat, for a count of seven.

- Pause for a count of two.
- Repeat the in, out and hold pattern of breath. The sound of your breath will be like the ebb and flow of the ocean. The length and speed of your breath is controlled by your diaphragm.

Practise this for as long as feels comfortable, working up to about 10 minutes each time you do it.

5.

CARE
Be gentle with yourself

Goddess comes to tell you to take care of yourself. She sees that you have been so busy 'doing' that you have forgotten how to 'be'. You have been spending so much time doing what you think will please others that you have forgotten how to please yourself! Remember that you are a human being, not a human doing. Today's Western world is so much about achievement and competition it is easy to get swept up in the maelstrom of working towards goals and expectations. When you are in this state your ego takes hold and bats you around like a ball. Your ego needs approval and validation from others and you can feel only as good as someone else's opinion. Goddess is here to say it is time to get off this rollercoaster!

She calls you to be still, to connect with Her love within you and to remember that Her love for you is unconditional. It is not dependant on your achievements; She does not love you less if you didn't get that job, lose that weight or burn that dinner! Goddess cares for you whatever happens and longs for you to care for yourself too. She is here to guide you to that still place within yourself that is unaffected by whatever life brings. This inner stillness will bring you confidence and peace. It will make you impervious to storms and allow the spirit of caring and love to flow freely in your life.

💜 *Goddess-inspired daily practice:* sit comfortably. Visualise being somewhere peaceful and quiet and wait for a visitor. This visitor represents a part of you that is wounded and needs care. When they arrive, let them introduce themselves, invite them to sit with you and ask them what they need in order to be healed. Let them speak. Listen with full attention. When they have finished telling you their story, give them care and empathy. Allow them to stay just as they are or perhaps they will take themselves off somewhere.

This process of self-care can be very healing. However, some visitors may require a great deal of care and empathy to be healed and this can take time and emotional strength.

You may like to make space for a different visitor day by day, until in time no one will come and you will have a sense of peace and completeness.

6.

COMPANIONSHIP

You are not alone

Goddess comes to tell you that you never need
to feel lonely for She is always with you. She
manifests Her love in all of creation. All beings
are connected and in this way Her love can flow
like a river from one to another through people,
animals, plants, trees and elements. Goddess is
here to remind you that your place in the chain
is vital! Even on the days when you feel as though
you have nothing to give, just by existing you have
played an essential part.

She comes to remind you of the value of companionship. She encourages you to find some way today to show another being some love: a smile, a hug, a friendly gesture, a compliment or kindness. If you know someone who seems like they need a companion, consider going out of your way to be friendly to them. Goddess needs the weakened links to be strengthened by kindness and amity.

She may send Her sacred creatures as prompts or guides to help you make the right decisions and remind you to tune into your intuition. Badger may be sent to remind you of the importance of family and kinship. Fox may indicate you need to become more aware of those around you and pay attention to their behaviour. Is there a subtle message you are missing, a cry for help or a gift being offered? Don't miss them. You are not alone. You share this beautiful planet with all of Her creation and She longs for all of Her beings to love and care for each other.

💜 *Goddess-inspired daily practice:* pay extra attention to all the beings who enter your life. Soften your vision and quieten your mind, and focus on your heart and theirs. Listen for the feelings and needs that are going on within you and them. Try to connect with them from your heart. Be open to allowing companionship and loving connection into all of your relationships, especially the ones that are fragile or challenging.

7.

COMPASSION
You are loved unconditionally

Quan Yin, the Chinese moon Goddess of mercy, comes to you with the gift of compassion. Compassion is the state of being that can transform the world. For that transformation to take place the flame of unconditional love must be lit in all hearts. Myth tells us that Quan Yin attained enlightenment, but just as She was about to enter heaven's gate She paused and, hearing the cries of the world, She decided to return and help humankind find the right path. She comes to say that to love others you must first love yourself. She teaches that every breath in is an opportunity to experience the sensation of self-love and self-acceptance, and every breath out is an opportunity to release what no longer serves you.

Quan Yin knows and understands your sorrows. She soothes your sadness with Her balm of unconditional love. She asks that you practise seeing yourself free of suffering and at peace. Let Her light the flame of unconditional love in your heart so that you know what it is to love and accept yourself and all fellow beings and wish only the best for all.

♥ *Goddess-inspired daily practice:* this is a loving kindness meditation. Sit comfortably in a posture of peaceful intent. Close your eyes and focus on your breathing. When you are ready focus on the words: 'May I be safe. May I be happy. May I be filled with loving kindness.' After practising this for a while you can open up the flow of love and compassion by saying as many times as feels right: 'May all beings be safe. May all beings be happy. May all beings be filled with loving kindness.'

8.
CREATIVITY
Seize the day

Goddess of spring brings you Her gift of creativity. She comes to light your fire of passion and enthusiasm. Perhaps you have been feeling a lack of focus or direction. Open your arms, for Goddess brings you hare energy! Rest with Her sacred creatures for a short while and let them act as Her messengers. Hear Her telling you to prepare for a dramatic increase in activity in your life. Hare spirit will give you the drive to leap forward and the self-belief to follow your intuition and heart, for the seeds that have been sown are ready to burst through the soil and unfurl their soft green leaves. Bring the dreams, hopes and plans you have been nurturing into the spotlight of your attention and be ready for them to come to fruition. Just as Fire Goddess warms the earth in spring, so She will warm your creative desires. She calls to you to seize the day; it is full of possibilities just for you!

💜 *Goddess-inspired daily practice:* write down this simple question on a piece of paper: 'This time next year I would like to be known for creating ...' This does not need to be something physical. Leave the paper on a clean and inviting surface, and then take yourself off for a long walk. When you return home, make sure the first thing you do is write and let your pen be guided by your inner intuition. Once you are certain you have answered this question fully, now write: 'What can I do today to begin this change?' Once you have answered this question, make your dream a reality. There is no time like the present. Be courageous and become the change you seek in the world.

9.
DEDICATION
Your challenges will reap rewards

Lady Blackthorn comes to you offering protection. She is here to give you support if you feel you have been or are being misunderstood. Perhaps you long to live your life differently and you find that the things that are important to those around you do not resonate for you. You long to speak to the trees and animals and practise the olde ways, when people lived in harmony with and attuned to their natural environment.

Lady Blackthorn hears you. She is strong and wise and may teach you Her magical ways if you are ready to learn. However, She is a hard task mistress and will ask for your devoted dedication. Her teachings may not be easy. She may challenge you and ask you to face some dark truths. Just as Her bare branches in spring give forth precious sweet blossoms, so out of darkness comes light. And though Her fruit is bitter it is full of healing properties, so your challenges will reap reward. The way ahead may be twisty and unknown but you will not be alone; Lady Blackthorn will guide you. She will show you how to protect yourself so you will be strong and safe. She will help you let go of your negative ways and teach you how to be the best and most wondrous version of yourself. Are you ready?

💚 *Goddess-inspired daily practice:* dedicate a small part of each and every day to spending time in a meaningful place for you. Perhaps this is a space in a woodland, at the top of a hill, beneath a particular tree or it is a shrine in your own home. Sit in this space each day and bring your attention to your breath and your body. It is a task that is so simple, yet it is one that takes dedication to practise every day. If life circumstances mean you have to travel away from your spot, let your heart guide you to the nearest one. If you know your day is going to be extremely full, ensure you get up earlier or stay up later. This is a dedication to your connection with Goddess and yourself and harmony with the natural world. Notice that some days the connection will be distant or feel absent and on other days it will flow powerfully or feel like a familiar and old friend. Whatever your experience, do not be disheartened: your presence alone shows dedication and dedication is the entry price for self-compassion. Your practice is not a sprint, it is not even a marathon; it is a river that flows eternal.

10.

ENLIGHTENMENT

Let Goddess light fill you

Be still sweet one, for Goddess comes to enlighten
you. There are times when darkness seems to
envelop you but do not be afraid, for out of the
darkness comes a light that is brighter than you
have ever known. It is the light of Brigid's fire. It
is the fire of passion, creativity and courage, the
fire of the forge that can transform and create. It is
the fire with a centre of pure white light, a place of
serenity and peace. Goddess calls you to give Her
your darkness so Her fire can consume it.

Give Her the parts of your life that need reshaping and She will transform them. Let Her power enlighten you. Her pure love is ever expanding. Feel yourself embraced by its light and let Her lead you back to the source.

The ancient sacred symbol of the mandorla (also known as vesica piscis) in this picture represents balance, union and creation, and the spirals are a symbol of the expansive abundance of Goddess and also your journey back to Her. Look out for these symbols in your life and know that Goddess is always with you, guiding you back to the light. Even in your darkest moments, remember that the divine flame of Goddess perpetually burns in your heart. Call to Her and She will tend the flame, causing it to burn ever brighter to enlighten your spirit and fill you with love.

💜 *Goddess-inspired daily practice:* sit comfortably on a cushion or chair and place one hand upon your tummy and the other on your chest. After several minutes of rhythmic breathing, begin to envision letting a bright healing light into your body. Notice how and where the light wishes to enter into your body and where it travels within your body. Become aware of the properties of the

light: its brightness, heat, colour and anything else. With
your out breaths pay attention to releasing any darkness
from your body. If it is useful, let the light push out the
darkness, clearing it away in its own unique fashion.
Spend as long as you wish in this practice, focusing on
the light that spreads more and more within your body.
When you are ready, finish this exercise by opening your
eyes and bring the light sensation you carry with you
into the rest of your day.

11.

FLOW

Let Goddess blessings enrich your life

Lakshmi comes into your life to tell you that there is enough! She is Goddess of spiritual and material prosperity and wealth. She may be here for you now because you are feeling a sense of lack. Perhaps you fear a lack of love, happiness, money or time. Whatever it is, Lakshmi is here to tell you that there is an abundance of all that you can possibly need. She is depicted with four arms representing the four goals of human life: dharma (right way of living), kama (pleasure of the senses), artha (purpose) and moksha (self-realisation). Her lower left hand is manifesting coins of prosperity, while Her lower right hand is held in a position that offers the blessing of deliverance from fears.

She is showing you that you may be creating the lack by damning the flow of life's abundance and closing your eyes to the richness of its beauty. For instance, if you long to see the magnificence of the starry night sky you must first go outside and look up. It may be cold and you may need to wrap up, but if you make the move you will be rewarded.

Lakshmi longs to reward you for all the times you have done your best and all your acts of kindness, respect, care and love. She asks only that you allow Her blessings to flow.

💜 *Goddess-inspired daily practice:* dedicate time to getting into nature, even if it is an indoor environment with some plants. Sit still for a while and bring your attention to the sights, sounds and smells that come to your notice. Pay attention to the things that are so small you would not normally see them. Become aware of things on a large scale and how each living thing lives among the others. Bring your attention and curiosity to your senses and your environment and resist the desire to use your thoughts and intellect to judge, evaluate or understand. Try to experience the environment as if for the first time like a young child. At the end of the practice thank yourself by saying internally: 'I am not just my thoughts, my body or my emotions. I am the witness and I notice the beauty in the world and in me.'

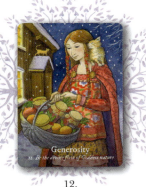

Generosity
12. *Be the divine flow of Goddess nature*

12.

GENEROSITY

Be the divine flow of Goddess nature

Goddess asks of you what you have to give. She comes with Her gift of abundance. She asks you to let go of your feelings of lack and your worries of scarcity. She says: 'I am everything. Align yourself with My flow and you will have all that you need.' She asks you not to hoard, hold on or block the flow, for generosity is love and by giving you are opening yourself to the divine flow of Goddess nature. She shows you what it is to truly give when She sees those who feel unseen and hears those who feel unheard, when She heals those who are sick and when She gives Her love to those who have forgotten how to give it to themselves.

Follow Her guiding light and be generous with your time, your kindness and your material things but most of all your love. She will reward you with so much more. Give with the joy of a child feeding the ducks. Give with the abundance of waves spilling into rock pools. Give with the spirit of the air rushing into your lungs. Give, give, give with this energy and you will find you are always full and never empty. Trust in the generosity of Goddess love.

💜 *Goddess-inspired daily practice:* today, find some way of showing your generosity. It may be as simple as a smile to someone who seems sad, a phone call or message to someone to say some kind or loving words, a gift of your help or time or forgiving someone who has wronged you. Remember that the object of your giving is not to receive gratitude, thanks or even an acknowledgement. You are not the benefactor of this gift but the channel through which divine energy is flowing. Goddess sees what you do and She will reward you with Her love.

Harmony
13. Perfect balance

13.

HARMONY
Perfect balance

There is no light without dark, no up without
down, no life without death and no summer
without winter. Goddess holds the wisdom of
perfect balance. She has conducted the universal
orchestra in exquisite harmony since the dawn
of time. You are one of the musicians in that
orchestra. Are you being attentive to Her baton?
Are you living your life in a way that creates peace
and harmony? Can you sit in the darkness knowing
that it will pass and the light will come? Can you

accept the low times in your life without anger or blame and know that happiness will take its place?

Goddess is here to tell you to listen and watch with your intuition and your heart to the subtleties of life's rhythm and play in harmony with it. When you learn to do this you will find you are no longer swimming against the current but flowing in harmony with life. Take yourself out into nature and attune yourself to the changing seasons. Learn from the wisdom of the trees: they blossom when it is time to blossom, they fruit when it is time to fruit and they rest when it is time to rest. They do not waste their energy in fighting what they cannot change.

Look into yourself. Is there a part of you that is struggling to be in the harmony of the world right now? Do you feel out of balance? Goddess is here to help you find ways to harmonise your life and redress the balance. She calls you to reconnect to the love that moves and touches all things in this vast interconnection of universe. Let go of trying to bend, shape and carve the world to your design. Go with the flow and know that Goddess has it all held in perfect harmony.

💜 *Goddess-inspired daily practice:* sit in a comfortable position with your back straight. As far as possible, let go of anything that happened before this moment and anything that you have planned for after this time. Close your eyes and slowly repeat the mantra 'I choose to let go' to yourself three times. Consciously release any tension you are holding anywhere in your body (and particularly in your shoulders, face and jaw). Let it go. Feel as though you are being gently pulled upwards from the base of your skull. Begin to follow your breath as it comes in and out. Listen to the sound it makes, and see if you can notice the point at which the inhalation becomes the exhalation, like the crest of a wave. Let yourself tap into that place of peace and harmony that exists in the core of your being. Continue to watch your breathing as it flows in and out for about two minutes. Gently wiggle your fingers and toes and open your eyes.

14.

HOPE
Out of darkness comes light

Demeter, corn Goddess and loving Mother, is the
keeper of the sacred law, the cycle of life into death
into rebirth. She knows the sorrow of loss and the
joy of reunion. She knows that each have their time.

Her beloved daughter Persephone was stolen
away into the underworld and Demeter was
distraught. In Her anguish the power of Her gift
of fertility to the land weakened and the plants
withered and died. Eventually Demeter discovered
Persephone and was overjoyed; however, Her

beloved daughter had eaten some pomegranate seeds while in the underworld, which meant that She could only return to her mother for half of each year. During the other half she would have to return to the darkness of Hades' world. While Persephone was away Demeter's tears washed over the land; Her sorrowful sighs and moans were the winter storms and Her loneliness laid the earth bare.

Demeter comes to you now, saying: 'I understand. I hear you when you call for help. I know that there are times when life can be hard. But I also know that the darkness is balanced by the light. Loss and sadness are real and when they consume you it feels that they will never go. But everything is always changing, just as Persephone's return brings the spring and winter's time is done. Hope will take the place of sadness and flowers will bloom again.'

💜 *Goddess-inspired daily practice:* within the next 24 hours, find or make a special symbol or token for yourself that you can carry with you. This is your talisman for hope; let it be the reminder that darkness can only exist because of light. Take your token with you as you go into your days. When things are going well hold it and give thanks, charging it with gratitude and positivity. If you stumble upon a rough patch when things are difficult for you, again reach for it and feel the good vibrations that you have charged it with and let it be a reminder that good times will come again.

15.

IGNITE
Release your potential

Wake up; wake up! Do you hear Her call? Brigid is here to relight your inner flame. As a young child your light shone so brightly, and life was full of possibilities and potential. But as you grew up the challenges and setbacks you experienced have dimmed your light. Perhaps things feel less possible now and the road ahead seems steep and strewn with boulders. Fear not, for Brigid comes to you now bringing Her flame of passion, courage and power. It can ignite your zest for life; it can fill you with enthusiasm, love and joy for life; it can make you feel like a child again!

Just as nature rests during the winter months and reawakens in the spring, you too can emerge from a dark place and step into the light. Brigid's spark can relight the fire of potential within you. Let Her guide you. To begin with She may encourage you to make just small changes in your life, but like the tiny buds that appear on barren branches in the spring there is huge potential in these small things! Her inspiration can light your way ahead, allowing you to think in a creative way and opening the door to wonderful possibilities. Brigid is offering you the flame of love. Are you ready to love your life?

💜 *Goddess-inspired daily practice:* at the beginning of each day write down 'Today I will use my Goddess-gifted passion, courage and power to ...' and then journal your response. Focus on just one thing. It may be something new or an ongoing project, or perhaps concluding something that has been left unfinished or letting go of a negative habit. Write down how your passion, courage and power will help you to succeed in your task. At the end of the day make notes on how your powerful focus has helped you in your productivity.

16.

JOURNEY
Your life is a sacred gift

Goddess is here for you to tell you that all is well.
You do not need to worry or stress that you are not
on the right path or that you are not as far along as
you think you should be.

Let go of your uncertainty and fear about what
you should be doing with your life. All this will
dissolve with a shift in your consciousness. Realise
that life is a journey of discovery, of yourself and
of the world. There is nowhere to get to but right
here and right now. Treat each moment as though

it is the most precious gift, as indeed it is, or your life is a sacred gift. Instead of looking outside for a destination, journey deeper within yourself.

Let go of tirelessly searching for the right way, the noble way, as if some narrow and winding trail will lead you to a higher realm if you could only find it and be worthy of walking its path. Clear your vision and realise that your way is the right way, and because you are at this place at this moment in time it is the perfect place for you to be.

Goddess witnesses your journey for She is the divine within you that has brought you to this moment. She sees and loves you as you are right now. You are your journey, moment by moment, breath by breath. Stop looking for your path outside of you because you are it!

💜 *Goddess-inspired daily practice:* whenever you encounter resistance towards a task, notice if you are telling yourself that you 'should' be doing it. This may indicate that you are not following your heart but rather pushing towards an external goal that is not enriching to your soul's journey. Take time out to reconnect with your breath and your body and Goddess will guide you in your quietness. Always be true to yourself.

17.

JOY
Embrace the blessing of life

Freya, Norse Goddess of love, brings you Her gift of joy. She asks only that you open yourself to Her and She will fill you to brim! Her joy is boundless and Her love is fathomless.

Freya knows the secret through and through and comes to share it with you. She knows that life can also bring challenges and hardships; She has seen the difficulties, sorrows and burdens you have had to deal with and She comes to give you permission to put them down.

Just for today, set aside your sadness, your worries, your concerns, as they will still be there if you choose to pick them up again; instead, open your arms and your heart to the flow of love and joy that Freya brings you. Let it be like a soothing balm on your wounds; it will surely lighten your load. As your load is lightened so Her heart is filled with more joy, and She will keep topping up your heart with that flow of joy. Goddess knows that you were born to shine. You are a unique and beautiful creation and She longs for you to really know the joy and blessing of being alive.

Even if you are feeling disconnected from Goddess, the miracle of your being is seen and known by Her. Perhaps you are not ready to rejoice quite yet. Do not worry; all is well, for Goddess knows when you are ready to open your heart to Her and that is enough. Your willingness is your gift to Her, and She will clear the way ahead. Perhaps you may not return for your heavy load, choosing instead to skip, dance and jump for the sheer joy of being alive! You may choose to step into your future with Freya's gift of joy and witness the miracle of creation in all other things. And perhaps you may pour your joy into all living beings and notice that your heart is always full to the brim.

💜 *Goddess-inspired daily practice:* sit in a comfortable position. Relax your body and bring your attention to your breath. Follow it as it flows in and out in a natural and unforced way. Consider the feeling of joy and happiness. Think of someone you know well and love who is happy and successful. Wish them more happiness and joy. Do the same for someone you have no strong feelings for: wish them happiness and joy. Think of someone you have problems dealing with. Apply the same feelings of wishing them joy and happiness. Even if you have trouble doing this stay with it, wishing them happiness and joy. It is the intention that is important even if the feeling is not quite there yet. Finish the meditation by coming back to your breath and feeling your body's weight on the chair or floor.

18.
LOVE
Be free from all that holds you back

Rhiannon, Goddess of love and sensual pleasure, comes to you now saying: 'Feel Me now as lover. I am life's lust, I am pure love.' Her white mare may gallop into your dreams. Will you ride her through the swirling veils and into the otherworld? Are you ready for transformation, from caterpillar to beautiful butterfly, from duckling to magnificent swan?

She has come to show you the power of love. She is love and She changes everything She touches.

Let Her love teach you to live from your heart and to love and embrace your beautiful body. Hers is a path of deep connection. She calls you to open to Her sacred fertile power. Let Her move you if you are stuck. Let Her hold you if you are afraid. Let Her heal your wounds and make you whole.

Now is the time to cast aside your limiting thought patterns. Stop making negative judgements and criticism about yourself and others.

Rhiannon is here to set you free from all that holds you back. Her gift of freedom is love! The waves of change are coming. Are you ready to ride Her white horse and crest the waves with love?

♥ *Goddess-inspired daily practice:* take away mirrors, remove magazines, websites, mobile apps or anything in your life that projects bodily image. Use the next week for exploring the feelings and sensations in your body without the illusion that love and pleasure are purely physical. Spend time listening to your body and hearing what it is asking for without judgement. Treat your body with all the kindness it deserves. If you find yourself getting caught up with having to look a certain way, bring your attention towards a pleasurable sensation you notice within you instead. Your body is beautiful, so use this week to really feel and honour it.

Love your body
19. Let your beauty radiate out

19.
LOVE YOUR BODY
Let your beauty radiate out

The Hindu Goddess Rati delights in Her unique
beauty and calls to you to do the same. You are
divinely gifted with sensual sensitivity, and Rati
encourages you to find pleasure in these sacred
gifts. Divine feminine energy flows in you; let that
energy be expressed and felt with delight. You are
divine beauty, your body is a miracle of creation.
Let Goddess express Her wonder through you.
Take care of your beautiful body; it is a miracle of
creation. There has never been a body like yours

before and there never will be again. No other human has a body that has seen, felt, touched, tasted or heard in quite the same way as yours.

Rati is here today because it is time you celebrated the miraculous gift that is your body, your own unique vessel for exploring the richness of the world. Develop a friendship with your body: listen to it, give it what it needs, thank it for all it gives you. Recognise and tune in to the reality that your energetic body does not stop at your skin. Your subtle energies radiate outwards into the world. Loving your body is the best gift you can give to Goddess, yourself and everyone around you.

💜 *Goddess-inspired daily practice:* each day choose a sense to focus on and give that sense a treat. Be filled with gratitude for this sacred gift. One day you might choose the sense of touch. Become more aware of sensation on your skin. Perhaps treat yourself to a massage or gift a friend or partner with a massage, relishing in the gift of touch. Another day treat your sense of smell by vaporising some essential oils or taking a scented bath. Treat your sense of taste with a delicious meal, savouring each mouthful by eating slowly and without distractions. Let your sense of hearing be indulged by an evening of listening to your favourite music. Dim the lights, make yourself really comfortable and let the music fill your being. Take yourself out into nature to treat your sense of vision. Let the Goddess-gifted colours of the natural world lift your spirits and be filled with gratitude.

20.
NURTURANCE
Restore your balance

Is there an aspect of your being that has been calling for your attention? Goddess comes to you today asking you to check in with yourself. Are your mind, body and spirit in balance, or is there one part of you that you have been neglecting? Perhaps your pursuits in life have led you to nourish and care for two of these elements while the other one has been left behind and forgotten. Goddess restores the balance in all living things. She is here to guide you back to harmonious balance.

Without nurturing the mind, the spirit and body will not have knowledge and wisdom to steer their choices towards compassionate conclusions in a complicated world. Without nurturing the body, a keen mind and enriched spirit will be trapped inside a vehicle that does not serve them well. Without nurturing the spirit, the mind and body will be unable to connect with divine love and beauty and life will feel hollow and futile.

Goddess longs for you to feel whole and complete. Are you nurturing every aspect of your being? Be still and listen; Goddess will guide you. Once you have recognised which aspect of your being needs more attention, give it all the care it needs. Take small steps and be kind to yourself. Feeding the parts of yourself that have been forgotten may take patience. In the fullness of time your mind, body and spirit will resonate as one. Nurture yourself and your balance will be restored, so that you will be in harmony with yourself and the flow of life.

💜 *Goddess-inspired daily practice:* having established which aspect of your being needs more care, write down in your journal some ways that you might nurture it.

For example, for the mind, perhaps make time for more reading or consider taking a course. For the body, try a gentle yoga practice, exercise session or walk each day. For your spirit, perhaps try a daily meditation practice, spending time in nature or simply making time to be still and allowing Goddess to unfurl your spiritual wings.

21.

PEACE
Open your heart

Goddess brings a message of peace, asking you to put down any grudges you may be holding. Look out for signs and symbols She may place in your life to encourage you to stop and reflect on any negativity or even hatred you might be nurturing towards yourself or others. She asks you to open your heart and let Her in. Her peace and love can transform anger into empathy. She points the way towards quiet spaces where you may hear Her guiding voice more clearly. She will help you find compassion and peace in your heart and give you the gift of wishing for peace within the hearts of others, so that where you once saw enemies you now can see friends.

You may carry with you the wounds of past relationships that may not have worked out in the way you liked. Goddess says She will heal your wounds but the scars will remind you of the life you have lived. With peace in your heart you will find that you can look at the scars but feel no pain.

Goddess wishes you peace in your thoughts so you can notice moments when you think of yourself as anything less than perfect and replace those thoughts with love, or when you think of others with negative judgement you can direct your thoughts towards loving kindness for all. Goddess wishes you peace in your words so that your internal and external language will speak messages without criticism, judgement, blame, comparison or envy but only with a voice of love and compassion. Goddess wishes you peace in your heart so that your body is free from the aches, pains and discomfort that comes from carrying messages of suffering. You are filled with a lightness of being, an openness and playfulness that is one with the world and all beings within it.

Goddess says it is time now to let go of burdens, grudges and envy and let peace fill the spaces in your being they once occupied.

Goddess-inspired daily practice: use the affirmation 'Today may I have peace in my thoughts, peace in my words and peace in my heart' and notice how you experience these wishes. You may like to repeat these words as a mantra and/or write them in your journal.

22.

PROTECTION
Goddess has your back

Arta (or Artio; Artha) is the great She Bear Mother Goddess. She is fiercely protective of you, Her child. Know that you are always safe under Her watchful gaze. She is nurturing and gentle but also powerful and strong. She is Ursa Major, the great She Bear in the night sky. Call on Her now if you are in need of strength and resilience, or if you are in emotional, spiritual or physical discomfort. If you find yourself in a dark place, reach out for Her. She knows every corner of your dark cave. Although it may be fraught with fear, in the darkness She may show you the power of your own inner strength. Her deep breathing may still your bat-winged panic and fill you with a deep inner peace. When you are ready to leave the cave, feel for Her warmth. She may ask you if there is anything you would like to leave behind and then She will lead you through the winding passages and out into the light. Her love will soothe and nurture your soul.

She has always been with you and stands by you today. Her love is unwavering. When you find yourself in a challenging situation, when your heart is racing with fear, when you feel you just can't cope, remember She is right behind you, warm and strong. She nurtures you and guides you. Reach for Her and She will calm you, protect you and fill you with Her unconditional love.

❤ *Goddess-inspired daily practice:* sit quietly and close your eyes. Breathe in for a count of two and out for a count of four. Repeat three times. Now imagine you are out for a winter walk. You look down and see a little bird in the snow. It is frightened and cold. You pick it up gently and hold it softly against your heart, keeping

it warm. Your warmth and love restores its strength.
You set it down and it gives you a look of thanks before
ruffling its feathers and flying off. Hold on to this feeling
of love and compassion and now apply it to yourself,
holding your hands over your heart as you drink in this
warm maternal Goddess-gifted love. Sit with this feeling
for as long as you like.

23.

RADIANCE
Rejoice in your life

Flora is here to take you by the hand and lead you into the sunshine where you belong.

No more hiding in the shadows, no more silencing your voice and no more walling up your heart. Goddess comes to say it is time to rejoice, be expansive and radiant.

The sunflower tilts its head towards the power of the sun and it does not fear standing taller than other flowers. The birds sing as loudly as they can and trees stand proud in the splendour of their growth. Flora comes to say 'It is your turn now!' It is time for you to find your voice so that you can speak the truth in your heart. It is time to own your Goddess-gifted beauty, to celebrate your body and rejoice in your life!

Listen to your heart's desires and know that all things are possible. Step into your dreams and make them real; don't be afraid to shine. There maybe those who stand in the shadows and fear your power to step into the light and who will envy the song in your voice and the grace of your movement. Their time to shine will come, but right now it is your time. Flora rejoices with you and gives you the courage you need. There is nothing to be gained by hiding in the shadows just so others won't be dazzled by your light. Instead, your light will give them the courage to make the move themselves.

Let each of your days have song, movement and passion. Rejoice in the power of your body. Celebrate the delights in this world. Express the desires within your heart. Shine with the light of Goddess love and step into the radiant being you were born to be!

💜 *Goddess-inspired daily practice:* in your journal write down your dreams and desires. Make a vision board with images of how you would like your life to be. See yourself as the most magnificent version of yourself. Reflect on what you can do to manifest your joyful future. Find things in your day that make you smile and do things that make you happy. At times this might mean stepping away from the status quo or other people's expectations of who they imagine you to be. But this is the new you! Have courage and stay with your intention of living your life as brilliantly as you can.

24.

RE-ALIGNMENT

Feel the ebb and flow of life

In the turmoil of life it is easy to be carried away on a current that is taking you away from where you want to be. Mother of Water comes to help you swim back into the flow of divine alignment. Life is a sea of energetic forces pushing and pulling; if you feel battered and bruised and as though you are gasping for air, Goddess is here to guide you to still waters. Feel Her soothing touch. Let Her help you find practices and ways of being that will keep you centred. She will re-align you. Mother of Water knows what it is to ebb and flow. If you are aligned with the push and pull you can flow with it, strong and unscathed. Your body is energy; listen to its natural rhythms and remember to flow with them.

Goddess may send you a guide in the form of one of Her water creatures. Seal may come into your life, perhaps in your dreams or as a picture, sculpture or in the flesh. In whatever form it comes to you Goddess will be reminding you to pay attention to your deep inner feelings, your imagination and intuition.

Goddess-inspired daily practice: no more fighting with yourself. Create time in your day or in your spiritual movement or breathing practice to hold and notice the uncomfortable emotions and thoughts that may arise. Be aware of the discomfort and accept it for what it is; perhaps it is sadness, regret, shame or guilt. Welcome it with compassion, for you are the host and it is merely a passing guest. In its own time it will move away from the spotlight of compassionate attention and float away as a cloud. Dedicate time to using the power of noticing, accepting and compassion for whatever arises for you each day during your daily practice. If at times tears flow or the body needs to rock or move, let it do so. Move with the tides of emotion and feel their flow. In time you will notice they are only the waves and not the depths of the entire ocean.

25.

REBIRTH
Let go of the ties that bind

Be still, dear one, and rest. There is a time for
being busy and there is a time for being still. For
there to be harmony in your life you need to allow
times of quiet withdrawal from the demands of this
fast-paced world. Step into Her dark cave and Wise
Grandmother Goddess will be there. She will hold
you in your stillness. Let Her float you through
lifetimes past, memories and dreams. She will paint
Her promise of devotion on your heart and hold
you safe. Surrender to Her all your feelings of pain,

shame or guilt. She can cut through all the binding ties that hold you in self-doubt and limitation.

She is here to restore you, to heal the bruises, the disappointments and the heartaches that life has brought. Take time to be with Her. She has known you since before you were born and watched over every faltering and surefooted step of your way. She wants only the very best for you. She knows just how perfectly beautiful you are! She longs for you to remember to spend time with Her. Remember to be still and feel Her loving arms around you. Let Her embrace, restore and heal you so that you can emerge from the cave with joyful purpose as though re-born.

💜 *Goddess-inspired daily practice:* dedicate time either after waking or before going to bed for stillness. Remove all distractions so you can have as much time as possible undisturbed. You may want to walk in nature or meditate. Set the intention to notice any emotions or feelings that are present within you. Hold each emotion in your awareness and say quietly to yourself: 'I acknowledge you and I accept you are here.' At the end of your practice, take a moment to thank yourself for the wisdom and energy you discovered from being still.

26.

REFLECTION
Healing transformation

Goddess brings you corvid blessings. Her
magical crows are here with their energy of
transformation for you. If your life has been
stagnant and you have been feeling stuck and
uninspired fear not: with Goddess's crows to
guide you all is about to change!

On their dark iridescent wings they can take
you to places you have not ventured before,
and from these places you will gain a whole new
perspective on your life. You will be able to see how

to remove blockages and find new solutions to old problems that have troubled you for years. Crow Mother sees what is holding you back and longs to set you free. She cautions you, though, that change and transformation can be challenging and sometimes painful but the rewards will make it all worthwhile. She will be here for you and Her crows will guide you.

Take time to connect with Her in deep reflection. You may be taken to some dark inner places where healing is needed. Her magical crows will teach you to be aware of subtle changes in energy. Let divine wisdom guide you to whatever form of healing you need. Her crows will lead the way, showing you a different way of seeing. Take off your blinkers and see the whole picture. Let the creative, playful, inventive corvid energy into your life. Crow Mother is here to give you your own iridescent wings to fly.

💚 *Goddess-inspired daily practice:* take yourself a little out of your comfort zone, venturing to wilder places or in wilder weather. Take your movement or meditation practices beyond your usual length or intensity, paying attention to different people and saying 'yes' more often.

If stagnation creeps in, take the first smallest step to shift it. Stand up, put on your trainers, play some music that does not reflect your current mood and move or dance even if you don't want to. Lean into the discomfort; don't let it lean into you. It is in these moments that inspiration and creativity dwell, and procrastination and emptiness will be strangers to your home.

27.

REST
Be still and listen

Goddess comes to tell you to rest. Resting is vitally important, as you are not a machine but a beautiful bundle of exquisitely interactive energies. Each part is dependent on the other and each needs to rest. Sometimes the greatest progress is made during times of inactivity. This may be progress in the form of self-understanding and alignment with your soul's calling. Don't see resting as empty time but as precious time. It is time that you are giving in gratitude to your creator. Goddess will appreciate your gift!

Listen to your body and heed its needs. Just as all of nature rests during the winter so it can flourish again in spring, so you need time to restore and recharge. Be interested and attentive to your physical and energetic body. Times of rest give you the opportunity to acknowledge your own beauty and your own pain or suffering, which will in turn give you the understanding to offer unity and empathy with others. This is what the world needs.

Be aware of and tune into the changing seasons. Goddess speaks to you through the cycle of the wheel of the year. In a state of rest you are more receptive to Her. Earth Mother calls for you to weave yourself back into the web of life She creates. Rest and feel Her loving heartbeat in the land.

💜 *Goddess-inspired daily practice:* take yourself out into nature. Find a tree with a strong trunk, and stand with your back against the tree and close your eyes. Imagine you are merging with the tree. Feel your roots deep in the earth and your branches reaching high up into the air. As you breathe in, feel the grounding energy rising up from the earth to your heart and then breathe that energy out through your branches and into the sky above. With your next in breath pull the healing light from above down through your branches to your heart, and with your out breath send that healing light down into the earth. Let the energy flow through you. Allow yourself to merge with the flow of life. Continue until you feel one with creation. When you have finished this practice, rest awhile with the tree before giving thanks for its support and sharing its gift of life.

28.

SAFETY
You are held

Goddess is here to tell you that you are safe.
You are always in Her arms. If you are feeling
vulnerable or afraid be calm, for you are not
alone. You are held in the grace of ancient Mother
Goddess. Her loving care nurtures you always.
Perhaps you are suffering adversity or difficulty in
your life. Divine Mother is here to soothe you and
give you strength. She assures you that you do not
have to achieve certain goals or look or be a certain
way to be worthy of Her love; it is completely

unconditional. This is pure love, the true vibration of life. When you tune into this vibration magical things happen!

If you ever encounter an adverse remark or negative comment, treat it like an unwanted gift and graciously refuse to own it for it will not sit comfortably in the vibration of love. Goddess gifts you Her colourful coat of love protection, which will always keep you safe. Glowing with Her love within you, you will find you are making decisions from your heart rather than your head. This will take you along unexpected paths and open doors that you had previously not seen. If you are ready for this new adventure open your heart and let love lead the way.

♥ *Goddess-inspired daily practice:* in your journal write a list of people who you feel safe enough to go to for advice or to ask for help. Reflect on the qualities of these people and how it is that you feel safe within their space and trust their words. Goddess leads Her children to be there for one another. These are the people who are vibrating at the same frequency as you and who will be able to support you in times of need. You will hear the words of Goddess through the mouths of your nearest friends. Be prepared to hear the truth, which may not always be comfortable, but what is being said is out of true love. Goddess has sent you an inner circle of people to support and protect you in this world. Take time to seek them out.

Sanctuary
19. Connect to your inner strength

29.
SANCTUARY
Connect to your inner strength

Mellangell, also known as Monacella, comes to you
through the mists of time to offer you sanctuary.
Legend tells us She was the daughter of an Irish
king and She fled to Wales to escape an arranged
marriage. She lived for many years in the remote
wilds in solitude. One day the prince of the region
was out with his huntsmen and dogs hunting
hares. The dogs were in pursuit of a hare but it
ran and hid in the folds of Mellangell's dress. The
prince and his men were stunned by this woman's

beauty and the aura of peace and sanctuary that surrounded Her. The dogs too were halted in their chase and could do nothing but bark at the hare as it stared boldly at them from the shelter of Mellangell's sanctuary.

Mellangell calls to you saying: 'You have all you need within yourself. I will give you the courage to stand strong against adversity and hold you safe. There is a well of peace inside you. Spend time sitting by this well: stare into its depths and you will see yourself as the strong powerful being that you truly are. When you get to know this truth it will radiate as love from within. I am Goddess and I am you! Feel Me within yourself and you will be your own sanctuary. I will send Hare into your life to remind you to seek safety in the stillness within yourself, where you will always find Me.'

> ♥ *Goddess-inspired daily practice:* if you can, spend time in nature during the next few days. Seek out places where you feel comfortable and safe. Repeat the affirmation to yourself: 'May I have peace of mind and ease of being.'

30.

SELF-DISCOVERY
Dive deep

Mistress of the Seas calls you to dive deeper into the emotional depths of your being and discover more about what lies below the surface of your being. Like the sea, your surface can belie what is actually going on below. She calls you to connect with your true feelings. Is there a turmoil of bubbling emotion that needs calming or a stagnant pool that needs clearing and cleansing? She urges you to have the courage to plunge beneath the surface level and discover what lies beneath. She will be there with you to help and guide you.

Who are you beyond who you think you are and who you say you are? This journey of self-discovery will help you clear away negative self-talk and living your life to please others rather than being true to yourself.

Goddess encourages you to explore deeper. On the ocean floor of your inner being there may be things hidden in the sand that need rediscovering and seeing with fresh eyes. Mother of Water will reflect bright sunlight on them and help you clearly see what needs to be forgiven and discarded and what needs to be thanked and treasured. Swim freely in your emotional depths and let Goddess reflect rays of sunshine. These may illuminate long-forgotten wonders and feelings of love that have been hidden deep in your underwater cave where no sunlight has shone for many years. Trust in this journey of self-discovery for Mistress of the Seas holds the chalice of emotional wisdom for you.

💗 *Goddess-inspired daily practice:* a lovely way to explore your emotional depths is to become more aware of your dreams. Keep a journal by your bed and jot down all that you remember about your dreams as soon as you wake up and before the dreams evaporate. You may find recurring themes and ideas. You might find it helpful to journal about your dreams, paying attention to the feelings that they evoke in you. Be gentle with yourself and explore with self-love and compassion.

31.

SHELTER
You are cherished

Winter Mother is here to tell you that you are seen, heard, loved and cherished. She holds you safe even in your darkest times and wraps Her arms around you. She wants you to know how much you are loved, always and unconditionally.

When times are tough, look, listen and feel for your Divine Mother. Sometimes She may be still and quiet, asking you to find peace within yourself. At other times She may stir and crash as a violent storm, teaching you to plant your feet firmly and hold on tight. In this way She may be testing your faith that She will always shelter you. And, like Her winds and rains, so too your dark clouds will pass.

In the depth of winter, although trees limbs are barren and bare, still their roots hold firm deep in the earth, connected to one another under the frozen surface. There is comfort and strength in connecting with others. Goddess asks you to reach out to soul sisters and brothers for support and kinship. She may guide you to find kindred spirits and send Her sacred creatures to lead you on your way.

Winter Mother says: 'I will hold you through the darkness and charge you with My love so that you will emerge from My shelter restored, bright and radiant.'

💜 *Goddess-inspired daily practice:* use every evening this week to write a short list of beautiful moments you have noticed today. They may be small events you witnessed in the natural world such as a pretty view or something you hadn't seen before on a routine walk. They may be in human relationships such as a kind gesture towards yourself or another, or they may even be the relationship you notice within yourself such as a moment of progress or change. Hold on to these lists, or continue writing them so they can be a witness to the presence of the Winter Mother's protection.

32.

SHINE
Hold your head high

Inanna has been honoured as Queen of the Sky since ancient Sumerian times. Later the Akkadians and Assyrians prayed to Her as Ishtar, the Phoenicians loved Her as Astarte and the Greeks as Aphrodite. Her power and strength lives on through millennia. She is Goddess of the bright morning and evening star. See Her shine. She comes to you now to remind you that you too are a bright shining light. You have Her timeless and limitless Goddess power within you. She sees you and knows how brightly you can shine.

Inanna stands Her ground with independent pride and asks that you do the same. Hold your head high and speak your truth. Look out for Her doves in your life; She may send them through the spirals of time to guide you. Do not give away the qualities that make you unique in an attempt to be like others and blend in. Inanna loves your uniqueness; that which makes you different is the essence of Her gift to you. Treasure Her gift. Let Her light shine through you. She will give you the courage to be your true self. Embrace your unique beauty and shine!

💜 *Goddess-inspired daily practice:* this is a morning practice to ground yourself. Stand up and place your feet flat on the ground, noticing the physical sensations of your body and the sensations of your feet connecting to the ground. Create symmetry in your body. It may be useful to visualise the energy of your body as a light around you that radiates outwards or to imagine roots from your feet reaching downwards and outwards into the ground. Through this posture you can set the intention to stand in your own truth and to hold your own sacred space. Carry this feeling of strength into your day.

33
SLEEP
Slow down

There is so much to fit into your life and
sometimes it feels that there is not enough time
to get it all done! You burn the candle at both
ends, and don't get enough sleep. Goddess is here
to say: 'Sleep is My precious gift to you. Be easy
on yourself and rest. Let Me speak to you in your
dreams. Let Me heal your body, mind and spirit
as you sleep.' Goddess encourages you to allow
enough time to sleep. Stop striving to get from
here to there, stop chasing rainbows and surrender

to the power of being instead of doing. In letting go you will find that inspiration will step in and what was an effort will flow with ease. Exhausted and depleted you will never reach that rainbow, but in dreams you may float on rainbow clouds of possibilities and learn new ways of being.

Sometimes sleep does not come easily. If this is the case Goddess encourages you to get out of bed and go into another room with dimmed light. Sit quietly and meditate, following your breathing gently in and out. Goddess will be there with you. Feel Her soothing your stresses away. Eventually you will be ready for sleep and can return to bed to journey through the night dreamscape with Her and wake refreshed.

💜 *Goddess-inspired daily practice:* gently ease yourself off caffeine and alcohol, particularly in the hours before sleep. Turn your bedroom into a holy temple for sleep. Keep the room clean and tidy and the bed pre-made. Remove all electronic devices (even your phone) and work material from your bedroom. Aim for between seven to nine hours of sleep.

One hour before bedtime, stop all work and screen activity and switch to light reading that is not work related. Before going to sleep you might like to write down five things you are grateful for that have happened during the day. Say the affirmation: 'Tonight I allow sleep to be my therapy. I allow my past to be released. I allow Goddess to show me my true beauty.'

34.

STILLNESS
Be calm and quiet

Goddess brings you the gift of stillness and serenity.
This is a very busy and noisy world, and it is hard
to find quietness either without or within. There
is so much stimulation. Perhaps your mind is in
overdrive with thoughts competing for space;
projects, plans, dreams and chores all clutter
together fighting for attention. Goddess has
come to you now offering peaceful stillness. She
understands that you are being swept along in the
hubbub of your world and comes to offer you Her

hand to pull you out of the frenzy. She calls you to walk with Her into a dream landscape where snow has stilled the chaos and hushed the noise. All is serenity and quiet.

She asks you to use this time to listen to what is within you, to let go of your feelings of having to do something, create something, appease someone or placate someone. Take advantage of the stillness and silence where movement, business, duty, obligation and noise cannot reach you. Like a rabbit deep within her burrow, retreat into the silence and safety. In the stillness Goddess asks you to hear the noise of the world babbling like a river beneath the ice. She calls you to listen with a heart free of judgement and full of compassion.

She may send Her sacred wren into your life to remind you to step off the treadmill from time to time so your voice and ideas can be heard more clearly from a place of refuge. Owl may come to show you that you may see the whole view more clearly from a distance, and Goddess may send you Her sacred dove with Her message of deep peace and stillness.

💗 *Goddess-inspired daily practice:* take time to sit in silence. In your mind's eye picture Goddess offering you Her hand and leading you into a beautiful snow-covered world. All is still and silent; the only sound is your breath. Follow your breath gently in and out for several minutes. Slowly follow Goddess into this peaceful world, listening to the scrunch of snow under your feet. She lays Her cloak onto the snow and invites you to sit next to Her. It is soft and warm and you lay your head on Her lap. Stay here as long as you like. When you are ready, get up and thank the Maiden for Her kindness and return to the present. Gently open your eyes. This is your place of peace that you can return to whenever life gets too hectic and you need stillness.

35.

WILDNESS AND FREEDOM

Let go and be

Elen of the Ways, Lady of the Wildwood, invites you to loosen your tight, cautious grip on life. Although it is prudent to keep your eyes open and check for danger, there is a fine line between caution and fear. Check in with yourself and ask: 'Am I walking my path with healthy carefulness or with anxiety?' Elen calls you to tap into the still, calm centre within yourself and be brave like a deer striding into a clearing just so she can feel what it is like to have the sunlight on her coat and see the blue sky above. Moving among the shadows is a safe way to watch for threats and stay safe and there certainly is a time for that. But now Elen is calling you to be wild and free! Step out into the open spaces, run and jump, skip and dance.

Lady of the Wildwood knows the magic that awaits you and She is beckoning you to step forward. She is encouraging your walk to become a stride and a stride to become a dance. Let the light illuminate you, and let your light illuminate others. Dance your dance, sing your song, dazzle with your brightness and become the wild and free spirit you were born to be!

💚 *Goddess-inspired daily practice:* identify and write down in your journal a time when you stepped away from a situation that could potentially bring you joy but that you felt was too difficult or uncomfortable. Having identified this time, now visualise yourself breathing in the spirit of Elen and stepping into that challenging situation feeling strong, sure footed and brave. Let Her wild and free Goddess energy course through your body and feel yourself come alive. Take this practice into your day and call to Elen when you need courage to deal with a challenging situation.

36.

WISDOM
Remember

Cerridwen, ancient Welsh Mother Goddess, comes
to you with Her teachings of wisdom. What is it to
be wise? How do you harness your wisdom? She
tells you that you came into this life as a wise being
and you have spent much of your time forgetting
and unlearning.

But fear not, for Goddess is here to guide you
back to remembering. She will teach you again
how to feel wisdom through nature, folklore,
stories and myths. She calls you to realise that

wisdom does not reside in the brain but in the heart.

Intelligence may be a path to wisdom but it is not the destination. In today's world when storytelling and the verbal sharing of olde ways is limited, books can be their substitute. Cerridwen encourages you to read fairy stories, folk tales, mythology and books about plants and trees, but most of all She calls you to go out into nature. Let the trees, plants and animals share with you their wisdom.

Goddess says She will come to you at significant times during your life to give you special opportunities to rediscover your inner wisdom. It is your decision as to whether to take them or not. She may come in many ways and sometimes Her teachings may be very challenging. Sometimes your spiritual growth may require you to upset the status quo of your life. You may decide to turn away and take an easier route; the choice is always yours. But if you long for Goddess wisdom in your heart and respond to Her call, She will always give you the love, strength and courage you need.

💚 *Goddess-inspired daily practice:* try this guided visualisation. In your mind's eye picture yourself walking into a woodland. You notice a particularly beautiful

big tree in a clearing and are drawn towards it. As you
approach you see there is an opening like a door in its
huge trunk and you peer inside. You see a spiral staircase
twisting downwards and you enter into the tree and
walk down and down. Your way is lit by candles in little
alcoves in the walls. At the bottom you find yourself in a
large room, also lit by candles.

You notice a shape at the far end of the room, and
as you draw nearer the shape becomes an old woman
dressed in black. She has an ancient wrinkled but kindly
face and is stirring a large cauldron. She looks at you
and says: 'Ah ha, you have come. Welcome my dear.' She
indicates for you to sit on a little wooden stool next to
Her. You sit with Her for what seems like a long time,
although you have no way of knowing. Although you
don't actually speak She seems to know what you are
thinking and answers your questions in your mind. You
feel wonderfully content. Eventually She looks up and
says: 'It is time for you to go. Thank you for coming, and
take this with you.' She gives you something significant:
it may be an action, some words of wisdom or a gift. You
give your thanks and return up the spiral staircase and
out through the opening in the tree and back through the
woods. You might like to journal about your experience.

ABOUT THE AUTHOR
AND ARTIST

Wendy Andrew lives, dreams and paints in the south of England surrounded by beautiful countryside and ancient woodlands. Her artwork is inspired and guided by the driving force of the divine feminine. She has been painting for almost all of her life, having been encouraged from a very young age by her artist father.

Wendy's spiritual quest has taken her along innumerable paths, and after many years of searching it was in nature that she heard Goddess whispering in the wind and vibrating through the land, saying: 'Here I am, feel Me in the turning of the seasons. I am maiden of spring, mother of summer and crone of winter. I am death and rebirth. I am you and you are Me.' From that time on Wendy has sought to share her love of Goddess through her paintings and writing.

Wendy also created the *Goddess Dream Oracle* published by Rockpool Publishing.

www.paintingdreams.co.uk